WHITE CROW

written by Shirley Frederick
collages by Susan L. Roth

HARCOURT BRACE & COMPANY

Orlando   Atlanta   Austin   Boston   San Francisco   Chicago   Dallas   New York
Toronto   London

White Crow had beautiful white feathers. His feathers were smooth and shiny.

Every morning he cleaned his white feathers. "I am the most beautiful bird in the world," he said.

3

Sometimes he would look at himself in a puddle.

When the light was just right, he could see tiny rainbows on his wings. "I am the most beautiful bird in the world," he said.

4

5

One day White Crow walked to his favorite puddle for a look. Something followed him. It looked just like him, but it was black.

When White Crow picked up his foot, Black Crow picked up his black foot. "Go away," said White Crow. "I am the most beautiful bird in the world," he said.

But Black Crow did not go away. He followed White Crow everywhere. So White Crow spread his wings and flew to his nest.

All night he thought about what to do. At last he had a plan. "I am the most beautiful bird in the world," he said. "I know just what to do."